Understanding Genetics™

Evolution

The Adaptation and Survival of Species

Kristi Lew

ROSEN
PUBLISHING®

New York

For Caroline—scientist, teacher, friend

Published in 2011 by The Rosen Publishing Group, Inc.
29 East 21st Street, New York, NY 10010

Copyright © 2011 by The Rosen Publishing Group, Inc.

First Edition

Library of Congress Cataloging-in-Publication Data

Lew, Kristi.
Evolution: the adaptation and survival of species / Kristi Lew.—1st ed.
    p. cm.—(Understanding genetics)
Includes bibliographical references and index.
ISBN 978-1-4358-9534-8 (library binding)
1. Evolution (Biology)—Juvenile literature. I. Title.
QH367.1.L49 2010
576.8—dc22

                                                                2009046684

Manufactured in the United States of America

CPSIA Compliance Information: Batch #S10YA: For Further Information Contact Rosen Publishing, New York, New York at 1-800-237-9932

On the cover: Over the last few decades, scientists have successfully unearthed many fossilized bones belonging to species related to modern humans. During a 2005 exhibition celebrating Charles Darwin, the American Museum of Natural History in New York displayed several examples, including these.

Contents

What hat do birds, bees, whales, walruses, horses, and humans all have in common? Well, for one thing they all share a common ancestor. This means that on the most basic level all these animals are related to one another. Animals are not the only ones that share the same origin. In fact, all living things can be viewed as branches on the tree of life.

There is a huge variety of life on Earth. Some living organisms, like bacteria, for example, are made up of only a single cell. Other living creatures, such as humans, have trillions. Life thrives all over the planet. Plants and animals can be found from pole to pole, in the water and out, and even miles underground. However, not all life-forms have survived. Dinosaurs disappeared from the planet millions of years ago. Woolly mammoths and saber-toothed cats followed. In fact, about 250 million years ago, scientists estimate that more than 90 percent of all the animals that lived on Earth at that time became extinct. Why did so many of them disappear? Scientists believe that one reason is that these species could not change, or adapt, to new environments quickly enough to survive. Today, many types of animals, from the gray wolf to the blue whale, are in danger of going the way of the dinosaurs.

Where did all of the plants, animals, and other creatures come from? Most scientists agree that all the

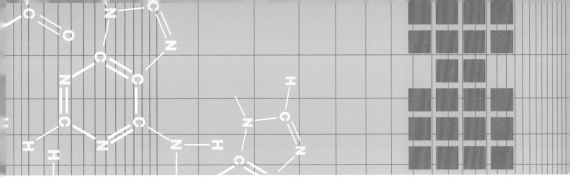

living things on Earth today originated from one common, single-celled ancestor that lived about 3.5 billion years ago. That means that all species alive today (scientists have discovered and described about two million species so far, but they believe there are millions more that have not yet been found and classified) are all related to one another—and to humans.

Long before Charles Darwin published his thoughts in his book *On the Origin of Species* in 1859, people noticed and wondered about the similarities and differences between life-forms. Darwin compared the way living things connect to one another with the branches of a tree. Today, that image remains. During Darwin's time, scientists relied only on the similarities and differences that they could see to decide how species might be related to one another. Today, scientists have much more sophisticated methods. They can study not only what they can see with the naked eye, such as an animal's anatomy, but also what they cannot see, such as an organism's genetic makeup. Advances in the science of genetics have helped scientists find connections between organisms. In turn, this has helped them develop a clearer image of how all the diverse life-forms on Earth fit into the tree of life.

The idea that all life-forms originated from a common ancestor and have changed over time into the variety of life that people see today is called evolution. This idea is supported by many scientific studies and observations. Some people like to point out that evolution is only a theory. It is true that scientists call it a theory. However, the word "theory" in science does not have the same meaning that it does in everyday speech. In casual use, the term

Mammoths, relatives of the modern elephant, disappeared thousands of years ago. To figure out what extinct animals were like when they were alive, scientists often study fossilized bones.

"theory" can mean "a guess or an opinion." In science, a theory signifies a well-studied explanation of observed and experimental data. Evolution, like other theories, has been subjected to many tests. So far, scientists have found nothing that would disprove the idea. Does that mean that the theory of evolution will never change? No, it does not. As with all scientific theories, the evolutionary theory is subject to change when new data becomes available. However, as of today, the theory of evolution is the best fit for the scientific evidence that biologists have observed so far. It is well accepted by most scientists. What makes these scientists so willing to accept the theory of evolution? To understand their reasons, people have to first examine how living organisms are related to one another.

CHAPTER one

Inheritance

One of the core ideas of the evolutionary theory is that all life started from one ancestor. Like branches on a tree, different species evolved from this one ancestor into the many forms of life that exist today. So just as you and your cousins share a common grandmother, different species as diverse as pine trees and elephants also share a common ancestor somewhere along the evolutionary pathway. Of course, certain living things are more closely related to one another than others. Certainly elephants, for example, have more in common with whales than with pine trees. Nevertheless, these organisms and all others are connected by an evolutionary link.

Many things change over time. Trees, for example, lose their leaves in the fall and their leaves grow back in the spring. A car abandoned in a field will rust away. People age and their looks change. However, none of these examples is an example of evolution. What makes evolution different is that it involves genetic changes within a population. These changes are passed down from generation to generation.

People in the same family often share some of the same traits, such as eye color, hair color, and height. These traits are determined by genetic information that is passed down from generation to generation.

Basics of Heredity

Your ancestors are the people in your family that have come before you, like your grandparents and great grandparents, for example. Each ancestor passed down certain characteristics to you. Some of these characteristics, such as hair color, eye color, and height, you can see with the naked eye. Others, such as blood type or the likelihood of developing a particular disease, you cannot see. These genetically determined characteristics are called traits.

A teacher explains deoxyribonucleic acid (DNA) using a model (right). Genetic information is passed down from one generation to the next in a chemical molecule called DNA. The DNA molecule looks like a twisted ladder, called a double helix.

Traits are passed down through families from one generation to the next. If your parents have dark hair, for example, you are likely to have dark hair, too. But this is not always the case. Sometimes a trait skips from one generation to the next. For example, instead of having dark hair like your parents, you might end up having bright red hair like your great aunt Ethel. No matter, the trait was still inherited from your ancestors. The particular combination of traits you inherited makes you unlike anyone else in the family. You are genetically unique, unless you have an identical twin. Identical twins are genetically the same, and, therefore, share many, if not all, of the same traits. Scientists call the combination of traits that a person has a phenotype. Many aspects of a phenotype can be directly observed. For example, if you have red hair, green eyes, and freckles, this combination would be considered your phenotype.

The chimpanzee is humans' closest living genetic relative in the animal world. The sequence of base pairs in human and chimpanzee DNA is nearly 96 percent identical.

Your phenotype is controlled by information present in almost every cell of your body. This information not only tells your body to make red hair, green eyes, and freckles, but also how to grow and function. The information is written in a code that your cells can read. It is stored in a chemical molecule called deoxyribonucleic acid, or DNA.

If you could see the DNA molecule, it would look a lot like a twisted ladder. The sides of the twisted ladder are made up of two chemicals—a sugar and a phosphate. Scientists also call these chemicals DNA's sugar-phosphate backbone. The rungs of the ladder are made up of chemicals called bases. There are four bases in DNA: adenine (A), guanine (G), cytosine (C), and thymine (T). The bases are always found in pairs. Adenine always pairs with thymine. And guanine always pairs with cytosine. So between the sides of the DNA ladder, there are rungs made up of two bases, called a base pair. Scientists have found that there are approximately three billion base pairs in the human genome. A genome is all the genetic material in an organism.

Passing Information Along

Some of the DNA base pairs work together in very long groups. These groupings of base pairs are called genes. The order, or sequence, of the DNA base pairs in a gene tells the body how to make chemicals called proteins. Proteins are very important in determining what a person looks like and how the body functions. The three billion base pairs of the human genome seem to be divided into about twenty thousand to twenty-five thousand genes. With the exception of identical twins, everyone's base pair sequence is slightly different. This difference in the order of base pairs is what makes people unique. However, most of the DNA sequence is the same for all humans. In fact, scientists estimate

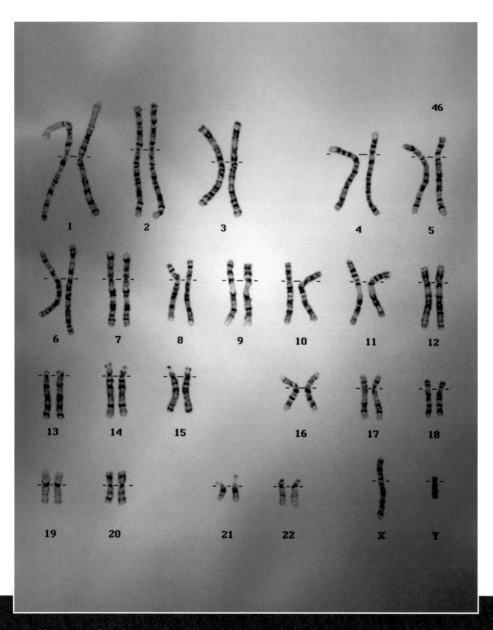

Most human cells contain twenty-three chromosome pairs. Twenty-two of these pairs, the autosomes, are nearly identical. The last pair, the sex chromosomes, may be made up of two X chromosomes if the person is female or an X and a Y chromosome if the person is male.

that an individual's DNA differs from all other humans' DNA by about 1 percent. Furthermore, a person's DNA is almost 96 percent identical to that of the chimpanzee, humans' closest living genetic relative in the animal world.

Zebra Fish and Human Skin Color

Studying the genomes of other animals can sometimes help scientists learn more about the human genome. A group of cancer researchers at Penn State University were doing just that when they found something surprising. At the time, they were searching for genes in zebra fish that they hoped might lead them to find cancer-causing genes in humans. Instead of cancer-causing genes, they discovered one of the genes that controls skin color.

The pigment that determines skin color is called melanin. People (and zebra fish) with dark skin colors have more melanin than people with light skin. The Penn State researchers found a mutation in the DNA of some zebra fish, called golden zebra fish. The change in the golden zebra fish's DNA decreased the amount of a protein needed for making melanin. With smaller amounts of this protein being made, the fish's body makes less melanin. The reduced amount of melanin makes the fish's skin color lighter than fish without the mutation.

Humans and zebra fish have some similar genes. Often, these genes have the same function in the fish and in people. This skin-color determining gene that the researchers found in zebra fish is one of them. They have since been able to find the same gene in the human genome. The sequence of the gene is about 70 percent identical in zebra fish and in humans.

In humans, scientists have found that the gene has two versions. People of African descent are more likely to have one allele, named the "G" allele. People of European descent have a different version, called the "A" allele. Only one DNA base pair is different in these alleles. But scientists have determined that these alleles are responsible for about 30 percent of the difference in people's skin color.

Genes are passed down from parent to child in structures called chromosomes. In most cells, humans carry forty-six chromosomes. Chromosomes come in pairs. Humans get one chromosome of each pair from their mother. The other chromosome comes from their father. Of the twenty-three pairs of chromosomes in a human, twenty-two are nearly the same size and carry similar genetic information. These chromosomes are called autosomes. The last pair is called the sex chromosomes. This pair of chromosomes determines a person's gender. Females inherit two X chromosomes while males inherit one X and one Y chromosome.

Some of the genes passed down from your mother and father are the same. But others are different. Different versions of the same gene are called alleles. For example, whether or not an individual has freckles is a genetic trait. There are two different freckle alleles. One allele tells the body to make freckles when exposed to the sun; the other allele tells the body not to make freckles.

The allele that tells the body to make freckles is the dominant allele. Dominant genes will show their effect in a person's phenotype even if there is only one copy of that gene. So if either parent passes on the gene that tells the body to make freckles, their offspring will have freckles. The version of the gene that tells the body not to make freckles is called a recessive gene. In order for recessive traits to show up in the offspring, both parents must pass down

These teens are siblings. Some genetic traits are controlled by a single gene. Scientists believe, however, that most traits are polygenic, or controlled by multiple genes. Skin color, face shape, and IQ are all thought to be polygenic traits.

the same recessive gene. Traits that people can see, such as freckles, make up an individual's phenotype. A person's phenotype is determined by the interaction of the genes on their chromosomes, or the person's genotype, and his or her environment.

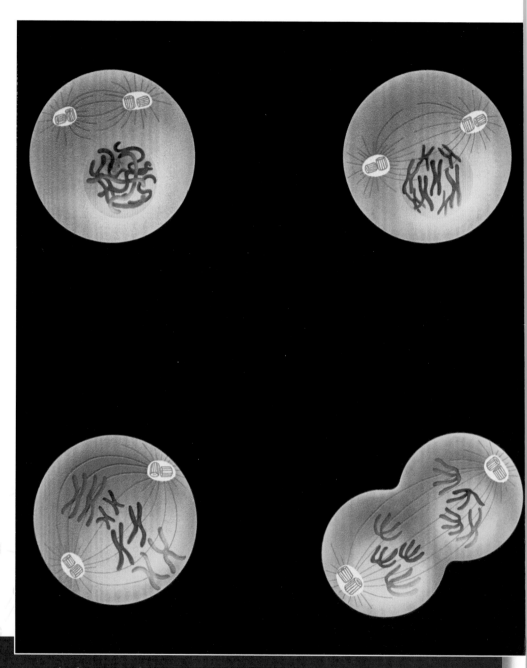

During the first stage of meiosis, chromosome pairs line up side by side. Sometimes the chromosomes in a chromosome pair will exchange some DNA. This exchange, or recombination, creates genetic variation.

Having freckles or not is controlled by a single gene. But not all traits are controlled by a single gene. In fact, scientists think that most human traits are controlled by multiple genes. They call these traits polygenic traits. The shape of your face, the amount of curl in your hair, your IQ, and your skin color are all believed to be polygenic.

Gene Shuffling and Mutations

Most cells in the human body have forty-six chromosomes in them. The only ones that do not are red blood cells, which have no nucleus and no DNA, and gametes. Gametes are reproductive cells. A female gamete is called an egg. The male gamete is a sperm. In humans, these cells contain only twenty-three chromosomes. During sexual reproduction, an egg fuses with a sperm. The resulting cell has forty-six chromosomes and, if all goes well, it divides and grows to become a child.

To produce cells with half the number of chromosomes, gametes must go through a process called meiosis. Before meiosis begins, each DNA molecule is copied. As a result, instead of one twisted ladder of DNA, each chromosome contains two identical twisted ladders of DNA. (Scientists call the twisted ladder shape a double helix.) Now the cell has twice the usual amount of DNA. During the first phase of meiosis, each chromosome pair (one from the mother and the other from the father) lines up side by side. Sometimes they exchange bits of DNA. This swapping of genetic material is called recombination, or crossing-over. Recombination creates a huge opportunity for genetic variation. Genes get shuffled around on chromosomes and a large number of possible gene combinations can be produced. This gene shuffling is what causes siblings to look different, although similar. Brothers and sisters have some genes in common and these genes make them resemble one another. But they also have some genes that are different, which makes each of them distinct.

As a cell continues through the stages of meiosis, the chromosome pairs are pulled apart and two daughter cells are created. This division reduces the number of chromosomes in each daughter cell by half. Because of recombination, each daughter cell has a unique DNA sequence. But, at this stage, the chromosomes in the daughter cells still consist of two double helices of DNA, twice the amount of DNA needed. To reduce the amount of DNA, each daughter cell goes through another division. During this division, the two double helices of DNA that make up each chromosome are pulled apart. The result is four daughter cells with twenty-three chromosomes, each consisting of a single double helix of DNA with a one-of-a-kind sequence.

Random combination of gametes and recombination both increase genetic diversity in the offspring. However, these are not the only means of genetic variation. Mutation can cause a permanent change in DNA, too. Changes in the DNA sequence may be caused by a copying error during cell division. Other changes may be caused by conditions in the environment, such as exposure to radiation or chemicals. If the DNA is damaged in a body cell, the mutation cannot be passed on to the next generation. But if the mutation occurs in a gamete, the new DNA sequence can be passed down from parent to child.

What does all this information have to do with evolution? A change in frequency, or commonness, of a particular allele in a population over time is how a species evolves. However, scientists have not always known about DNA, chromosomes, and alleles. This understanding arose over many long years.

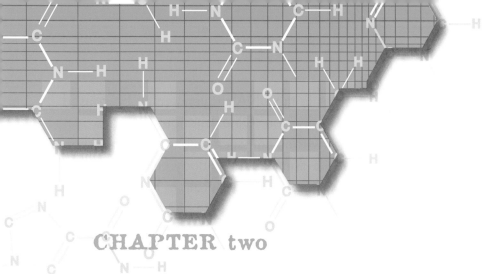

CHAPTER two

History of Evolutionary Theory

There is probably no better-known scientist in the field of evolutionary theory than Charles Darwin (1809–1882). But Darwin knew nothing about DNA, base pairs, and genes. Genetics, as a science, was developed long after Darwin's death. Nor did Darwin really come up with the idea of evolution. In fact, early Greek philosophers such as Aristotle also believed that current species gradually arose from a common ancestor.

What Exactly Is a Species?

In the late eighteenth century, the French naturalist Georges-Louis Leclerc, comte de Buffon (1707–1788), developed the definition of the term "species" that is still used today. A species is a group of organisms that can produce fertile offspring. In other words, members of the same species can have young together and their young can also reproduce. Different members of the same species may look very similar. However, they might also look very different. Consider dogs, for example. A Saint Bernard and a dachshund look very

This illustration of dogs (mastiff and shepherd) is from the Comte de Buffon's 1852 book about the natural history of animals. Some types of dog look very similar, whereas others do not. Regardless of their appearance, if two individuals can produce fertile offspring together, they are part of the same species.

distinct. But, they are members of the same species. Scientists call their species *Canis lupus familiaris*. A Saint Bernard and a dachshund could produce puppies together. They might be funny looking, but the Saint Bernard–dachshund puppies could grow up and produce puppies of their own, too.

Early Evolutionary Works

Charles Darwin was not even the first Darwin to come up with the idea of evolution. In 1794 and 1796, his grandfather Erasmus Darwin (1731–1802) published a two-volume book called *Zoonomia*. This book outlined Erasmus Darwin's ideas about the natural world. In it, he suggests that all animals could have come from one

Evolutionary Dead Ends

Some animals look like they are members of the same species, but they are not. They may even be able to produce offspring together. But they are not really the same species because the offspring they create cannot reproduce.

Horses and donkeys, for example, can reproduce. The offspring of a male donkey and a female horse is called a mule. The offspring of a female donkey and a male horse is called a hinny. However, horses and donkeys are not really the same species. Neither mules nor hinnies can have babies. Both animals are sterile.

The reason mules and hinnies are sterile has to do with the number of chromosomes in their cells. Horses have sixty-four chromosomes. Their gametes have half of that number, or thirty-two chromosomes. Donkeys have sixty-two chromosomes and their gametes have thirty-one. When the parent's gametes are fused during fertilization, the resulting cell has sixty-three chromosomes. Having an uneven number of chromosomes is not a problem for the growing mule or hinny. However, when it comes to making gametes, the uneven number of chromosomes is a problem. None of the gametes that are produced has a full set of chromosomes, which is needed to form offspring.

ancestor. It is considered one of the first formal theories of evolution. By studying domesticated animals and observing wildlife, he developed the idea that some animals were more likely to survive and reproduce than others. This idea would later be expanded on by his grandson, who called this process natural selection.

Another naturalist, Jean-Baptiste Pierre Antoine de Monet, chevalier de Lamarck (1744–1829) of France, published his main work on evolution in 1809. Lamarck proposed that organisms that were put into a different environment adjusted to their new situation. Those organisms then reproduced and passed on the new, helpful trait.

Jean-Baptiste Lamarck believed that giraffes that were forced to reach high into the trees to find food permanently lengthened their necks and then passed this newly acquired trait down to the next generation.

Charles Darwin would come to the same conclusion (that organisms evolved) thirty years later in his *On the Origin of Species*. However, Lamarck and Darwin differed in their explanation of how this process occurred. Lamarck believed when an animal's environment changed, its needs changed. These different needs caused the animal to behave differently and use its body in different ways. Lamarck proposed that if an animal used a body structure or organ more, that structure or organ would grow larger. On the other hand, if the animal's new needs caused it to use a structure or an organ less often, the structure or organ would shrink. This is known as the use and disuse theory.

He also believed that these newly acquired traits could be passed down to the next generation. So, for example, according to Lamarck's beliefs, giraffes evolved to have longer necks because their environment changed forcing them to reach higher into trees to reach the leaves they needed to eat. Over time, Lamarck believed, the animal's neck would stretch. In addition, the giraffe's offspring would be born with a longer neck.

Lamarck also believed that evolution should be viewed more like a ladder than a tree. In other words, Lamarck believed that the goal of all simple creatures was to evolve into more complex life-forms. Lamarck equated more complexity with being more "perfect." He did not believe that species became extinct. Instead, they evolved into a "better" species.

Charles Darwin

Darwin agreed with some of Lamarck's ideas. Like Lamarck, Darwin came to believe that species changed over time. However, he did not believe that Lamarck's use and disuse theory explained how species changed.

In 1831, at the age of twenty-two, Darwin was invited to spend five years on a British ship called the HMS *Beagle*. He was asked to

This watercolor of Charles Darwin was painted in 1840. Darwin is probably the best-known scientist in the field of evolutionary theory even though he was not the only, or even the first, scientist to come up with the idea.

go along on the voyage to keep the twenty-six-year-old Captain Robert Fitzroy company. The objective of Fitzroy's journey was to explore and map the coast of South America. The expedition was also to include a group of islands called the Galapagos Islands 800 miles (1,287 kilometers) off the South American coast. Darwin kept careful notes about (and drawings of) the animals and plants he saw on his trip. He also collected many fossils and specimens that he brought back to England to study later. He was struck by the similarities and differences of some of the plants and animals that he found on the Galapagos to those on the mainland of South America.

When he returned to England, Darwin started a systematic study of the specimens he brought home. In 1839, he published *Journal of Researches into the Natural History and Geology of the Countries Visited During the Voyage of H.M.S.* Beagle *Round the World*. This book, which is commonly known as *The Voyage of the* Beagle, described his general observations about the trip. However, he said nothing about his ideas of the evolution of species in this book. In fact, Darwin would keep his theory of how species change to himself for another twenty years. He was aware of how his controversial ideas would upset many people, including his wife, Emma.

The year after Darwin returned from his voyage aboard the *Beagle*, he read the work of British economist Thomas Malthus (1766–1834). Malthus proposed that the human population would grow out of control if there were no natural disasters, disease, and famine. This idea caused Darwin to wonder if the same notion was true of animal populations. Before this time, Darwin had assumed that animals produced only enough offspring to keep the number of animals in the population steady. After reading Malthus's views, however, he began to see that animal populations often produced more offspring than was needed. These offspring had to compete for limited food and resources and not all of those offspring survived. Quickly, Darwin realized that some of the offspring produced would

This title page, written in Charles Darwin's own hand, is from On the Origin of Species. *Darwin's most famous work described his ideas on the evolution of species and was published in 1859, more than twenty years after his voyage aboard the HMS Beagle.*

be better suited to survive their environment than others. Those that were better suited to survive would grow up, mature, and reproduce. In time, the traits carried by these survivors would become more common in the population. Darwin's theory of how species change over time is known as natural selection.

However, even this concept was not Darwin's alone. In 1848, another British naturalist, Alfred Russel Wallace (1823–1913), visited South America. As Wallace traveled through Brazil and the Amazon Basin,

Natural Versus Artificial Selection

Darwin and Wallace observed how selection of certain traits in the wild can drive evolution. Darwin also noticed that humans can influence evolution. Artificial selection occurs when people choose certain animals or plants for a particular trait. Dog breeders, for example, can affect the way different breeds look by choosing which dogs are allowed to mate with one another. In certain breeds, such as bulldogs and Pekingese, for example, flat faces are a desired characteristic. Therefore, breeders choose parents with the flattest faces in the hopes that their offspring will have flat faces. Chinese shar-peis, on the other hand, are bred for their wrinkles. This type of selection can also be called selective breeding.

However, unlike natural selection, selective breeding does not necessarily improve a dog's fitness. In fact, in some breeds it can cause health problems. The flatter noses of bulldogs and Pekingese can cause the dogs to have breathing trouble. Shar-peis are also more likely to suffer from skin infections because of bacteria growing in their wrinkles. Selective breeding can also cause other problems. Animals and plants bred for a particular phenotype often have genotypes that are more similar than the larger population. This similarity can lead to genetic disease as the number of recessive genes increases in the population.

he collected samples of plants and animals. Although Wallace's samples were destroyed in a fire on the way back to England, he and his observations survived.

In 1854, Wallace once again set out on an expedition. This time he traveled to the islands of Malaysia, where he stayed for eight years. While he was there, he compared the islands' plant and animal species to those of nearby Australia. The similarities between the species led him to believe that they were related, but their differences convinced him that they had evolved differently. Moreover, like Darwin, Wallace discovered and read Malthus's work. Based on his observations and reading, Wallace also developed the theory of natural selection independently of Darwin. In July 1858, both Wallace and Darwin published papers describing their theories. And in November 1859, Darwin's most famous work, *On the Origin of Species By Means of Natural Selection; or, the Preservation of Favored Races in the Struggle for Life*, was published.

Adaptation

In 1859, Darwin knew nothing of DNA and genes. Gregor Mendel (1822–1884), the "father of genetics," would not publish his research of inheritance "factors" in pea plants for another seven years. It would take nearly eighty more years before scientists discovered that Mendel's factor was the DNA molecule. However, Darwin did notice something interesting about some of the birds on the Galapagos Islands. In most ways, the finches on the islands looked very similar to one another. However, the size and shape of their beaks were very different. He noticed that finches that ate seeds on the ground tended to have large wide, flat beaks that were good at crushing seeds. However, the finches that fed on the prickly pear cacti had long, pointed ones. From their similarities, Darwin theorized that the birds were descendants of a common ancestor that was most likely from the mainland of South America.

Birds. Pl. 42.

Two cactus finches from the Galapagos Islands are seen in this illustration from the 1830s. While observing finches on the Galapagos Islands, Darwin noticed that the size and shape of the birds' beaks were very different depending on the type of food they ate.

As the birds spread through the islands, they adapted to different environments on different islands. An adaptation is a change that helps an organism become better suited to its environment. The cactus finch, for example, feeds on the flowers, fruit, and insects inside the flowers of the prickly pear cactus. The shape and size of their beaks helped the cactus finches benefit from a food source that other finches could not reach. From their original common ancestor, the Galapagos Island finches would eventually evolve into fourteen separate species.

In 2004, researchers at Harvard University identified the gene that determines the height and width of the finch's upper beak. This same gene is responsible for shaping the facial features of other laboratory animals, too. Two years later, the same research team discovered a different gene that controls the length of the bird's beak. By changing this gene in developing chicks, the scientists were able to show how different beak shapes could have formed at the genetic level.

CHAPTER three

Evolution of Populations

The blending of ideas from several different biological disciplines, from natural selection to genetics, to form today's theory of evolution is called modern synthesis. Over the years, many scientists have contributed to the combination of these ideas.

How Can a Species Change?

One of the scientists who helped advance modern synthesis was Ernst Mayr (1904–2005). In his book *Systematics and the Origin of Species from the Viewpoint of a Zoologist* (1942), Mayr proposed that a group of organisms separated from its main group by either time or distance could adapt in such a way as to eventually make the two groups incapable of interbreeding. If this occurs, a new species can be formed. If this process occurs because of a physical separation, it is called geographic speciation.

Consider, for example, that a group of coastal rabbits are happily living and breeding together. The rabbits are minding their own

Small populations, such as these members of the Old Order Amish community of eastern Pennsylvania, who do not exchange genetic material with the larger population are more susceptible to genetic drift.

business when a huge storm comes along and washes some of the rabbits out to sea. Luckily, the ocean-going rabbits are able to float along on some trees that were swept out to sea as well. Eventually, the marine rabbits wash up on a deserted island. Now there are two

Genetic Equilibrium

Natural selection, gene flow, genetic drift, the founder effect, and mutation are all ways that the frequency of an allele can increase or decrease in a population. In the early twentieth century, two scientists, Godfrey Hardy and Wilhelm Weinberg, proposed a mathematical model that explained how genotype frequencies change from generation to generation. This mathematical model has become known as the Hardy-Weinberg principle. The Hardy-Weinberg principle states that in a large population with random mating, allele frequencies remain constant in the absence of disrupting factors that could cause the ratio to change. This condition is known as genetic equilibrium.

For genetic equilibrium to exist, several conditions must be met, including the following:

1. *The population size must be very large.*
2. *Mating must be random.*
3. *All members of the population breed.*
4. *All matings produce an equal number of offspring.*
5. *Members of the population cannot leave and outsiders cannot get in.*
6. *There are no mutations.*
7. *There is no natural selection.*

If all seven of these conditions are not met, then the frequencies of alleles in the population will change. If gene frequency changes, evolution takes place by definition. Because it is extremely rare that all seven of these conditions are met, most populations are evolving all the time.

groups of rabbits. One is on shore and the other is on the island. These two groups can no longer mate with one another. It is too far to swim. The gene flow, or exchange of genetic information, between the two groups is cut off.

The environments that the two groups now live in are very different. The island rabbits adapt to their new environment. Maybe some of the rabbits adapt better than others. Over time, natural selection works on this group of rabbits. The ones that have best adapted to the food and climatic conditions on the island survive and reproduce. The others die out.

At the molecular level, the two groups are also evolving differently. Varying genetic mutations accumulate in the two distinct populations. For example, let's say that a mutation appears and spreads among the island rabbits. This mutation changes the rabbits' eating habits. The change in eating habits makes it easier for the island rabbits to survive on the island's plants, which are different from the mainland plants. The rabbits with this mutation have an advantage over the rabbits that do not have the mutation. They eat more food and the nonmutated rabbits start to die out. Over time, more and more baby rabbits are born with the mutation.

If, after several centuries of this isolation, another storm blows through and washes some of the island rabbits back to shore, they may once again encounter the mainland rabbits. However, if in their time on the island, the island rabbits have become too genetically different from the mainland rabbits, the two populations may not be able to interbreed. It is possible that the island rabbits have evolved new mating rituals. Or they may reproduce during a different season. Or maybe the two groups of rabbits try to mate, but produce no young. If any of these scenarios proves to be true, the two groups of rabbits have evolved into two separate species.

Gene Flow, Genetic Drift, and the Founder Effect

Natural selection is not the only way evolution occurs. Sometimes genetic variation is introduced into a population through migration. For example, consider two populations of lizards. One population

Natural Selection at Work

A clear example of natural selection at work is the case of the peppered moth. Before the Industrial Revolution occurred in England in the late eighteenth century, many of the native trees had light-colored bark. The peppered moth, which lived in the forest on these light-colored trees, was also a creamy, light color. The moth was very difficult to see against the tree bark. The moth's camouflage protected it from predators.

However, by the middle of the nineteenth century, coal-burning industries in the more industrial regions of England had covered the trees in soot, making their barks darker. The light colored moths, called typica, could be easily seen on these darker-barked trees. About that time, naturalists began to

notice another, darker form of the same moth. The scientists named this form carbonaria. The first sighting of a carbonaria moth was reported in 1848. Less then fifty years later, 98 percent of the moths around the industrial town of Manchester, England, were the carbonaria type. Because the carbonaria type was harder to see than the typica, they were eaten less often. Over time, the allele that produced the carbonaria type moth became more common in the population.

The darker-colored carbonaria type peppered moth is harder for predators to see than the light-colored typica type on soot-covered trees. Therefore, the frequency of the allele resulting in a carbonaria type moth increased dramatically during the Industrial Revolution.

carries the allele for green skin color. The other lizard population has brown skin. If one or more of the brown lizards moves to the area where the green lizards live and reproduce, the allele for brown skin color has been introduced into the population. The introduction of genes into a population due to the movement of an individual from one population to another is called gene flow.

The frequency of an allele in a population may also change if individuals with a certain trait and the alleles that carry that trait die or fail to reproduce, just by chance. Then only the survivors can pass their genes on to the next generation. If the population contained few individuals to begin with, the accidental loss of those individuals causes a measurable change in the frequency of the allele. Such random changes over time are called genetic drift. Genetic drift can cause evolution and speciation in a population. However, unlike natural selection, genetic drift does not select for better-adapted or healthier individuals. The process is entirely random and is notice-able only in small populations.

For example, consider a tiny population of lizards that contains both brown and green individuals. At first, assume that there are equal numbers of brown and green lizards. Then, during one generation, several of the green lizards are crushed by a falling boulder. Now the allele that controls green skin coloration is reduced in the population. Just by chance, the ratio of brown genes to green genes has increased. More individuals carrying the brown skin coloration have survived to have offspring. The change in frequencies of the alleles constitutes, by definition, evolution. Genetic drift reduces the genetic variation in a population.

The smaller the population, the faster the effects of genetic drift can be felt. If in future generations, for example, some other natural disaster should befall the small population of green lizards, the gene that produces green skin could be lost forever.

Another example of genetic drift is the so-called founder effect. The founder effect occurs when a small population, the "founders," starts a new colony in a different place, with the founders having one or more differences in gene frequency from the larger population as a whole. Because the founder population is small, distinctive alleles that they carry can, over time, be lost entirely through genetic drift—or they may increase in frequency, also by genetic drift. The Old Order Amish community of eastern Pennsylvania provides an example of the founder effect. These people are the descendants of about two hundred German immigrants that settled in the area in the 1700s. In this population of immigrants, some genes had a higher frequency than others. Because the Amish do not marry outside of their small population, the frequency of some genes has, by genetic drift, gotten even larger over time. For example, a recessive genetic condition, called Ellis-van Creveld syndrome, is much more common in the Amish community than it is in the general American population. This genetic condition causes polydactyly (extra fingers and toes), dwarfism, and heart abnormalities. Scientists have been able to trace the recessive allele that causes Ellis-van Creveld syndrome back to one couple that came to North America in 1744. The allele was passed down through generations of their descendants. As the offspring of this couple married and reproduced, the allele increased in frequency due to genetic drift. About one in sixty thousand to two hundred thousand babies are born with Ellis-van Creveld syndrome to people in the general population of the United States today. However, in the Old Order Amish community, one in two hundred babies is affected by the condition.

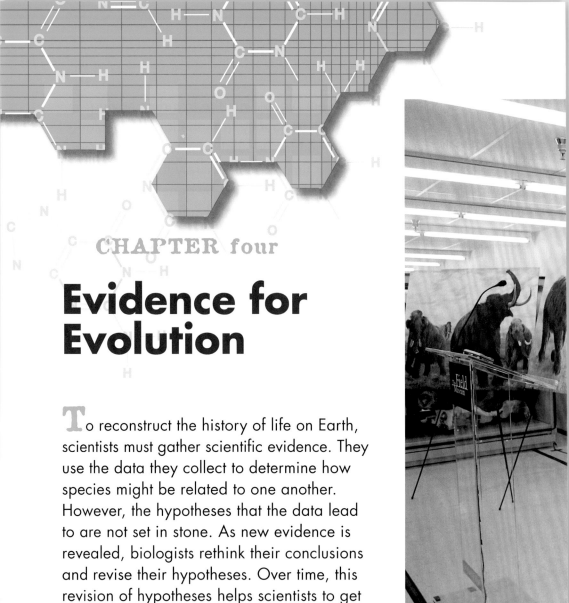

CHAPTER four

Evidence for Evolution

To reconstruct the history of life on Earth, scientists must gather scientific evidence. They use the data they collect to determine how species might be related to one another. However, the hypotheses that the data lead to are not set in stone. As new evidence is revealed, biologists rethink their conclusions and revise their hypotheses. Over time, this revision of hypotheses helps scientists to get a better picture of the way organisms are connected. To build the branches of the evolutionary tree, scientists gather data that may include physical traits, behavioral traits, or genetic sequences.

Fossils

One type of data scientists rely on to tell them the story of organisms that lived in the past is the fossil record. Fossils may be made up of

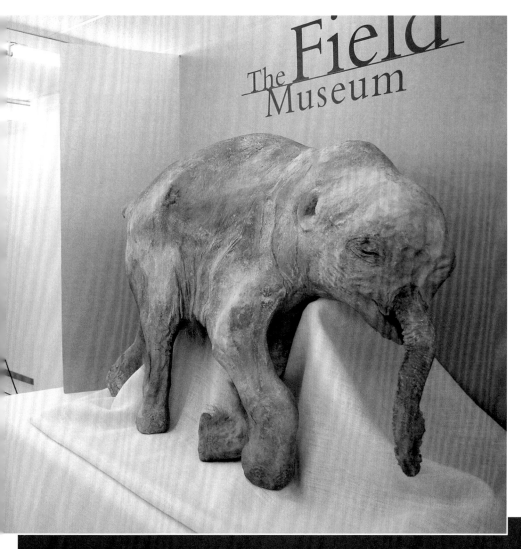

In 2007, scientists unearthed a well-preserved baby woolly mammoth from the frozen tundra of Siberia. It is rare that scientists find such a complete specimen to study.

an organism's actual remains, such as bones, teeth, or shells. Or they may be the remains of some characteristic of an organism's behavior, things like nests, footprints, or burrows, for example. By studying fossils, scientists can learn many details about the animals

Scientists have used the fossil record to trace the lineage of the modern horse back to a small, four-toed animal called Hyracotherium, which lived about fifty-five million years ago.

J. Brandstetter 97

and plants that lived on Earth thousands or even millions of years ago.

For a fossil to form, certain conditions must be present. And even if these conditions do exist, only parts of a plant or animal will likely survive to tell its story to generations of people millions of years later. Hard parts of the body, such as bones, teeth, or shells, are the most common parts that are fossilized. It is much more difficult for scientists to find soft tissue, such as skin or organs.

About three-quarters of the Earth's land surface is covered by sedimentary rocks. Sand, mud, or other sediments form a sedimentary rock. Over time, layer after layer of sediment settles on top of one another. The layers are pressed farther and farther into the Earth until, eventually, the bottom layers turn to rock. Sometimes a dead animal or plant gets caught in one of the layers and forms a fossil.

Occasionally, the conditions are just right and some of the soft parts of an animal's

Living Fossils

Some types of plants and animals have not changed in millions of years. Scientists call these organisms living fossils. Cockroaches, sharks, horseshoe crabs, ferns, tuatara, and cork palms are all examples of living fossils. The oldest fossil of a horseshoe crab, for example, dates back to more than four hundred million years ago. Its features have not changed in all that time. Cockroaches, the oldest living winged insect, have been around for about 350 million years. Both of these creatures roamed the Earth at the same time the dinosaurs did. So why did they survive and the dinosaurs did not? Because they were able to adapt to changes in their environment faster and better than the dinosaurs were.

This is a fossilized horseshoe crab that is hundreds of millions of years old. Horseshoe crabs that roamed the Earth 240 million years ago looked very similar to today's horseshoe crab. In all that time, the body shape of these living fossils has changed very little.

body might be preserved. In rare cases, even the whole body of an ancient plant or animal is found. For example, in 2007, scientists found a preserved baby woolly mammoth in the frozen tundra of Siberia. They estimate that the animal lived between forty thousand and ten thousand years ago.

Early naturalists did not want to believe that plants and animals could become extinct, or disappear forever. Therefore, when they found a fossil, they would try to make it match up with a living species. Even if they compared the structures in the fossil to that of a living organism and found differences, they would convince themselves that the fossil was just an unusual or misshaped specimen. Near the end of the eighteenth century, however, French scientist Georges Cuvier (1769–1832) showed that separate rock layers contained distinct types of fossils. He also showed that the deeper the rock layer, the more different the fossils were from living species. In general, deeper rock layers correspond to earlier time periods than those near the surface. Cuvier was very skilled at piecing together the animal skeletons he unearthed. He was also very good at showing how those skeletons were different from the animals that lived at the time. Using these differences, Cuvier was able to convince skeptics that some of the plants and animals that roamed the Earth had, indeed, disappeared forever.

Using fossils, scientists can attempt to piece together how life on Earth has evolved. They have, for example, traced the modern horse back to a four-toed animal that lived about fifty-five million years ago, applying fossil evidence. Fossils have shown that the earliest horse ancestor was about the size of a fox terrier. Scientists call this animal *Hyracotherium*. However, it is better known by the name eohippus, which means "dawn horse." Fossil eohippuses have been found in the western part of the United States and in Europe. The large tree of horse evolution contains at least fifteen different branches. Most of those branches lead to dead ends. In fact, *Equus*, the genus of the modern horse family, is the only surviving one. This branch of the tree developed about five million years ago and it is still going strong today. The modern horse family contains seven species, including the domestic horse, zebras, donkeys, and other animals.

Transitional Fossils

One criticism often used to discredit the use of the fossil record as evidence of evolution is the so-called missing link. A missing link is a fossil that shows characteristics of two different species. A fossil that shows the characteristics of a human and an ape, for example, would be a missing link. Scientists, however, prefer to use the term "transitional fossil" because the term "missing" implies that a fossil should exist but that it does not. Fossilization is an iffy process. Most organisms that

This is an artist's rendering of Tiktaalik roseae. Scientists have determined that Tiktaalik had features of both swimming fish and land-dwelling animals. Transitional fossils such as that of Tiktaalik give scientists a look into how different species may have evolved.

die do not do so under the conditions necessary for fossils to form. Therefore, scientists may never see these organisms in the fossil record. That does not mean that they did not exist. It just means that they were not fossilized. However, sometimes scientists get lucky and a transitional fossil is found. These transitional fossils can help scientists discover the evolutionary steps required for one species to evolve into a new one.

For example, scientists had long hypothesized that the first tetrapods, animals with a backbone and four limbs, lived in the water. They had evidence that the first land-dwelling tetrapod crawled out of the water about 375 million years ago. Scientists began to suspect that land-dwelling tetrapods may have evolved from animals called elpistostegids. These animals were large meat-eating fish that are now extinct. Researchers believed that these fish would have been a lot like today's alligators or possibly very large salamanders. For many years scientists looked for fossil elpistostegids to study. They did not find many and the few that they could find were not very complete.

Then, in 2004, researchers Neil Shubin, Edward Daeschler, and Farish A. Jenkins found a well-preserved elpistostegid fossil on Ellesmere Island in a northern territory of Canada. They named the fossil *Tiktaalik roseae*. *Tiktaalik* had scales and gills like a fish. However, it also had thick ribs and strong neck, shoulder, and wrist bones that could be used to prop itself up on land. Scientists hypothesize that these bones developed when *Tiktaalik* adapted to prey on fish in shallow water. In the process, the animal took on some of the characteristics needed to transition from a swimming fish to a land-dwelling creature. As a transitional fossil, *Tiktaalik* gives scientists a peek at the stepping-stones of evolution.

Tiktaalik roseae is not the only transitional fossil that scientists have found. In fact, one of the first, *Archaeopteryx*, was described about two years after Darwin's publication of *On the Origin of*

At first, scientists believed that this fossil of a previously unknown primate called Darwinius masillae, and nicknamed Ida, was a transitional fossil between lemurs and simians. The fossil is about forty-seven million years old.

Species. In 1861, an *Archaeopteryx* fossil was found in 150 million-year-old rocks. These rocks were formed during the late Jurassic period, the time when the dinosaurs lived. The fossil showed an animal with the teeth and long, bony tail of a reptile, but with the feathers of a bird. Many other fossils of feathered dinosaurs have been found since then, too.

In 2009, scientists unveiled what they thought could be another transitional fossil. This time the fossil was found in Germany's Messel Pit, a site that has yielded many well-preserved fossils. Scientists call the small, fossilized female primate *Darwinius masillae.* She has been nicknamed Ida. Ida lived about forty-seven million years ago. Originally, some scientists believed that Ida may have been one of the transitional fossils between simians (monkeys, apes, and humans) and a more distant lemurlike relative. Ida has hands that could have grasped objects, fingers that have nails instead of claws, and opposable thumbs (thumbs that can bend to touch the other fingers) like both simians and lemurs. But the rest of her skeleton is more like that of a lemur. Further studies have shown that Ida was probably a dead-end branch on the lemur part of the primate family tree rather than a close simian relative.

Homologies

Using fossils is not the only way scientists compare characteristics of related organisms. They also study homologies. Homologies can be discovered by comparing the anatomies of different species, studying similarities and differences at the cellular level, or studying vestigial structures.

By studying anatomy, for example, scientists have discovered that whales, bats, and humans all evolved from a common ancestor. The forearms of all these animals may look vastly different on the outside, but they look remarkably similar under the skin. Structures, such as a whale's flipper, a bat's wing, and a human's

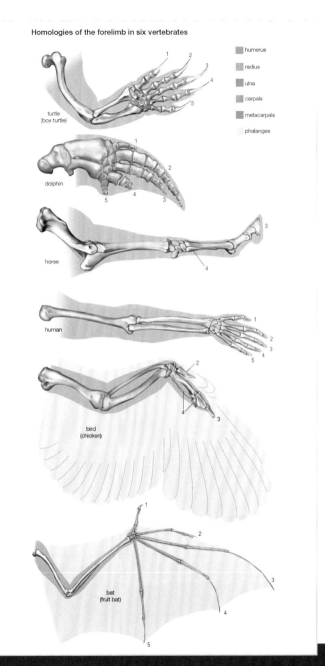

Homologies of the forelimb in six vertebrates

The limbs of turtles, dolphins, horses, and humans and the wings of birds and bats look very different on the outside, but are similar in structure. Structures that have similar anatomies but have different functions are called homologous structures.

arm, that have similar anatomy but different functions are called homologous structures. The prefix *homo* means "same." Organisms with homologous structures most likely shared a common ancestor somewhere in their evolutionary pasts.

Another piece of evidence that has convinced scientists that all living organisms have evolved from one common ancestor is the fact that, essentially, they are all alike. For example, all living beings are made up of cells. These cells have a cell membrane that contains a mix of molecules including lipids (fatlike substances that do not dissolve in water), proteins, and carbohydrates. Of these molecules, 99 percent are made up of only six elements. In addition, all plants and animals contain DNA. This genetic molecule is remarkably similar in all living things. No matter whether the DNA molecule is in a bacterium, a rat, or a human, it is still made up of a sugar-phosphate backbone and the four bases, adenine, guanine, cytosine, and thymine.

Vestigial Structures

Sometimes animals have homologous structures from a common ancestor that they no longer use. These body parts are called vestigial structures. Whales, for example, have leftover hind legs from when their mammal ancestor lived on land. Some snakes have hip and leg bones, too. Some types of fish and salamander live in completely dark caves. They are blind, but they still develop eyes. Even humans have a tailbone that they do not use.

Scientists also discovered how some of the structures inside the cell have evolved. Some of the earliest cells to appear on the planet were single-celled bacteria. Certain types of those primitive bacteria made their way inside more complex organisms. Indeed, they still live inside every living multicellular organism today. Scientists believe that a cell structure in animals (and plants and fungi and other multicellular organisms) called a mitochondrion and a structure in plants called a chloroplast started out as independent bacteria. Scientists believe this notion because these are the only structures in the cell that have their own DNA just as bacteria do. They also reproduce, copying their own DNA, just as bacteria do. Their DNA can be traced back to the bacteria that were their ancestors. At some point, these smaller cells came to live inside larger ones. This idea is called the endosymbiotic theory of evolution. Two species have a symbiotic relationship when they live and work together for the benefit of both species. And when one organism lives inside another organism and functions as a single organism, it is called endosymbiosis.

CHAPTER five

Evolution and You

Many people look at the evolutionary branch that includes humans and think that scientists are saying that humans have evolved from gorillas or chimpanzees. This belief is not true. What scientists are saying is that humans, gorillas, and chimpanzees all shared a common ancestor. This ancestor was not human. Nor was it a gorilla or a chimpanzee. Scientists also make no claims that humans are more evolved than gorillas or chimpanzees. Instead, humans, gorillas, and chimpanzees have evolved in different ways that are unique to each species.

Human Evolution

Modern humans have been around for about the last one hundred thousand years or so. Scientists call the group of bipedal (able to move on two feet) primates, which include chimpanzees, gorillas, and humans, hominids. The ones that belong to the human lineage are called hominins. Over millions of years, the hominin line

Homo neanderthalensis, *or Neanderthals, lived from 230,000 to 30,000 years ago. Their time on Earth overlapped with* Homo sapiens. *The first Neanderthal fossil was found in 1856, three years before* On the Origin of Species *was published.*

branched into at least twelve different species. However, today, only one remains—*Homo sapiens*, or modern humans.

The first hominin fossil to be discovered was found in 1856, three years before the publication of Darwin's *On the Origin of Species*. The skeleton was found in a cave in the Neander Valley of Germany. This early group of humans has become known as *Homo neanderthalensis*, or the Neanderthals. They lived about 230,000 to 30,000 years ago and their time on Earth overlapped with groups of *Homo sapiens* with more modern human features.

Thirty-seven years after the first hominin fossil was found, the first example of *Homo erectus* was discovered in Indonesia on the island of Java. Scientists nicknamed this fossil Java Man. *Homo erectus* are believed to have lived 1.8 million to 200,000 years ago. Since the discovery of Java Man in 1893, many other examples of *Homo erectus* fossils have been found throughout Africa and Asia. Scientists believe that *H. erectus* is likely the first hominid to have used fire.

In 1924, Raymond Dart discovered an apelike skull with humanlike teeth. This ancient human relative was given the name *Australopithecus africanus*. It had a larger brain than chimpanzees, but a smaller brain than modern humans. However, the specimen that Dart found was the skull of a child who was about six years old. Because of the similarities of a human child's skull to that of a young ape, his find was largely overlooked. Dart's discovery was nicknamed Taung Child.

Another reason Dart's Taung Child was basically ignored at the time was that it was very different from all the other fossils found so far. One of those fossils was called the Piltdown Man. Piltdown Man was unearthed in the Piltdown quarry in Sussex, England, by a lawyer and amateur geologist named Charles Dawson. The fossil appeared to have a humanlike skull and an apelike jaw. Dawson showed the bone fragments to Arthur Smith Woodward, the head of the British Museum's geology department. Woodward announced to the Geological Society of London on December 18, 1912, that

A scientist holds the Australopithecus africanus *skull, nicknamed Taung Child, which was found by Raymond Dart in 1925. Taung Child is believed to be about two to three million years old. Many scientists originally regarded the skull as an extinct ape species, rather than an example of an early hominid.*

the "missing link" had been found. Almost immediately, some scientists were skeptical. They argued that the skull and jaw were not from the same individual, but were actually separate human and ape fossils. But then in 1913, Woodward and Dawson found another fossil. This time the fossil had a canine tooth that was in between the size of an ape's canine and a human's. In 1915, the pair made yet another announcement. They had found more remains several miles from the original Piltdown site. The fossil molar and skull fragments appeared to be similar to those of Piltdown Man. This discovery was named Piltdown Man II.

However, in the 1920s and 1930s, many more hominin fossils were discovered, including Raymond Dart's Taung Child. These fossils had little in common with the Piltdown fossils. Indeed, as more fossils were found, it became clear that the Piltdown fossils just did not fit into the progression of hominin evolution as the other fossils did. Scientists were puzzled. At least they were until the late 1940s when chemical tests were developed that allowed the Piltdown Man fossils to be reexamined. What scientists discovered after these chemical tests is that the bones were not nearly as ancient as they appeared to be. Instead, the skull had been boiled and stained to make it appear as if it were as old as the gravel in the quarry. And the teeth on the jawbone had been deliberately filed down to make them look more humanlike. In 1982, scientists were able to determine that the jawbone actually belonged to an orangutan. The whole thing was a hoax. Exactly who decided to carry out the deception is not known. But once the Piltdown fossils were exposed as a fraud, the rest of the fossils found in the intervening years made more sense.

In the early 1960s Louis Leakey found the first fossil of *Homo habilis*. *Homo habilis* means "handy man." It was given this name because scientists believe it was the first hominid to use tools. The brain of *Homo habilis* was larger than the brain of any of the examples of *Australopithecus*, but smaller than the other *Homo* species. *Homo habilis* lived 2.4 to 1.5 million years ago.

The Leakey Family

Louis Leakey was not the only fossil hunter in his family. In fact, his wife, Mary, their son, Richard, and Richard's wife, Meave, have all had a large impact on the study of human evolution. Louis and Mary Leakey did most of their fossil hunting in the Olduvai Gorge in Tanzania. In 1950, when he was six years old, Richard made his first fossil find there, too. The little boy found part of a giant pig that is now extinct. In 1976, his mother, Mary, found some very exciting fossilized footprints. These footprints proved that, as Donald Johanson suspected, Lucy and other Australopithecus afarensis individuals walked upright on two feet. So far, the Leakey family has spent six decades trying to untangle the tree of human evolution. With the addition of Richard and Meave's daughter, Louise, three generations of the Leakey family have already made major contributions to science. They continue the search today, too.

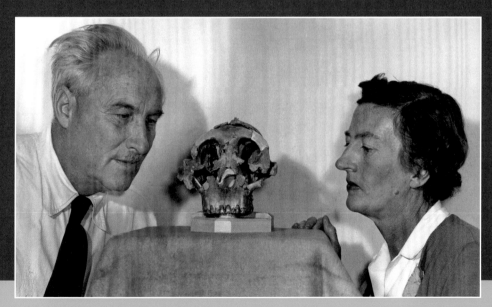

Louis and Mary Leakey made numerous important fossil finds in the Olduvai Gorge of Tanzania. Their son and his wife and daughter have decided to follow in the Leakeys' footsteps by working in the fossil-finding business.

In 1974, Donald Johanson found another important *Australopithecus* species. This specimen was given the name *Australopithecus afarensis* and nicknamed Lucy. Lucy was special because she lived about 3.2 million years ago. Her anatomy revealed to scientists that humans were walking upright on two feet at that time. In 1975, Johanson made another important find: the First Family. This group of fossils was found close to the same place where he had discovered Lucy. The bones belonged to thirteen people, but they were found all together. This was the first evidence that ancient humans lived in groups.

Then, in 2009, scientists made another big announcement. Between 1992 and 2009, an international team of scientists had discovered numerous fossils from a formerly unknown hominid species, called *Ardipithecus ramidus*. This primitive prehuman species lived about 4.4 million years ago, making it even older than Lucy. The most complete skeleton found was that of a female nicknamed Ardi. Like Lucy, Ardi walked upright when she was on the ground. However, her skeleton shows that she had feet that were more suited to climbing trees and a smaller

This laboratory drawer in Ethiopia contains several skulls of Australopithecus afarensis. In 1974, Donald Johanson found Lucy, the first A. afarensis specimen. Since that time, many other examples of A. afarensis have been found.

brain than Lucy had. Scientists are still working on exactly how Ardi and her kind fit into the human evolutionary tree.

Evolution and Your Health

When one species evolves into another through genetic changes over countless generations the process is called macroevolution. However, sometimes, as was seen in the example of the peppered moth in England, evolution does not take that long. When the frequency of a gene changes in a population over a relatively short period of time, the process is called microevolution. Scientists must use evidence, such as fossils, to try to piece together macroevolution. Even so, they can often observe microevolution taking place.

In 1928, Alexander Fleming discovered that bacteria would not grow near the mold *Penicillium notatum*. Fleming correctly reasoned that the mold gave off a substance that killed or slowed bacterial growth. He named this substance penicillin. Fleming had discovered the first antibiotic. Over the next several decades, scientists would find many other substances that would kill or slow the growth of bacteria and fungi. They used these medications to greatly reduce the number of deaths caused by diseases, such as tuberculosis and pneumonia, which are caused by bacterial infections.

However, bacteria have weapons of their own. They fight being wiped out. Some bacteria carry genes that make them resistant to the effects of antibiotics. When people take antibiotics, most of the bacteria invading their bodies die. However, the antibiotic-resistant bacteria survive. Then they reproduce. The frequency of the genes that allow for resistance to antibiotics increases in the bacterial population. Because bacteria can reproduce very quickly, evolution occurs rapidly. As a result, antibiotic-resistant bacteria have become a problem for people. When bacteria become resistant to a certain antibiotic, that drug no longer cures a person's bacterial infection. Some bacteria have become resistant to more than one antibiotic.

Overusing antibiotics can cause this problem to become worse. Therefore, antibiotics should be taken only when an individual has a bacterial infection. Antibiotics do not work on viruses. Taking them while a person has a viral infection, like a cold or the flu, not only will not help make that person feel better, but also will increase the frequency of antibiotic-resistant genes in the bacterial population. Not using all of the antibiotics prescribed by a doctor can do the same thing. It wipes out the susceptible bacteria and leaves behind the resistant ones to grow strong and more plentiful, possibly making the individual sick again.

The Importance of Biodiversity

Genetic diversity within a population is essential for its long-term survival. Without genetic variation, species may not be able to adapt to different ecological conditions. If a species cannot adapt, it will most likely disappear. When species go extinct, their disappearance decreases the variety of life, or the biodiversity, on Earth.

Human actions can have a huge impact on biodiversity. When people chop down forests to build houses, for example, they destroy the home of many plants and animals. The natural home or environment for a plant or an animal is called its habitat. Habitat destruction also occurs when humans claim grassland to create farmland or to build houses or businesses. When their habitat is disrupted in this way, most animals and plants do not have time to adapt to their new environment. If they cannot adapt, the plant and animal populations decrease. Therefore, there are fewer individuals left in the population in which to mate. Fewer breeding individuals lead to a smaller gene pool and less overall genetic diversity.

Reduced biodiversity can also spell trouble for humans. People get many of the things they need from the plants, animals, and other organisms around them. These organisms provide food, fiber, fuel, and medicines, for example. Scientists believe that there are millions

A lab technician works with a rosy periwinkle plant from Madagascar. The rosy periwinkle naturally produces chemicals that can be used in medications to treat lung and breast cancer. Today, the rosy periwinkle is endangered, mainly due to habitat destruction.

more species living on Earth today than the approximately two million they have discovered and described so far. Many of these species live in rainforests. Unfortunately, Earth's rainforests are quickly being destroyed. In fact, scientists think that humans are

losing from 1 to 137 plant, animal, and insect species each day because of the destruction of the rainforest. That adds up to more than fifty thousand species every year.

This habitat destruction destroys many beautiful life-forms. It could also destroy the hope of finding cures for many different diseases. Scientists have already developed 120 drugs from various plants. These medications are sold around the world today. But researchers have only had a chance to test about 1 percent of the rainforest's plants. What if one of the fifty thousand species lost to rainforest destruction this year could have been the ingredient for the cure of a deadly disease such as cancer or acquired immunodeficiency syndrome (AIDS)? If that plant disappears forever, humans will never know its potential benefit. Once a plant or animal species goes extinct, the possibility of it evolving into another species is also gone forever.

Glossary

adapt To change and become better suited to an environment.

alleles Different versions of the same gene.

autosome Chromosomes that do not determine sex.

chromosome A structure, containing genes, that is passed down from parent to offspring.

deoxyribonucleic acid (DNA) A large chemical molecule in nearly all cells that carries genetic information.

dominant gene A gene that will show its effects even if there is only one copy of the gene in the genome.

evolution The process by which populations change over time due to genetic changes.

extinct An organism that has died out or ceased to exist.

gametes Reproductive cells that have half the number of chromosomes as other cells.

gene A sequence of base pairs that tells the body how to make a particular protein.

gene flow The introduction of new genes into a population because of the movements of individuals from one group to another.

genetic drift A situation in which the frequency of alleles in a population changes by chance.

genetic equilibrium A situation in which no evolution is taking place.

genome All of the genetic information in an organism.

genotype The genetic makeup of an organism.

geographic speciation A situation in which a new species is formed because of a physical separation between a small group of organisms and the main population.

habitat The natural home or environment of a plant or animal.

hominid The group of bipedal primates that includes apes and humans.

homologous structure A structure with similar anatomy but different functions.

Glossary

macroevolution Evolution at the species level that occurs due to genetic change over generations.

meiosis Cell division that reduces the number of chromosomes in half and produces gametes.

microevolution Smaller evolutionary change that occurs due to genetic change over a relatively short time period.

mutation A permanent change in the order of base pairs in the DNA molecule.

natural selection The process by which organisms best adapted to their environment survive to reproduce.

phenotype Traits that can be seen or otherwise detected.

recessive gene A gene that will only show its effects if there are two copies of the gene in the genome.

recombination The process of gene swapping that occurs during meiosis.

scientific theory A well-studied explanation for observations and experimental data.

species A group of organisms that can produce fertile offspring.

trait A genetically determined characteristic.

For More Information

American Institute of Biological Sciences (AIBS)
1444 I Street NW, Suite 200
Washington, DC 20005
(202) 628-1500
Web site: http://www.aibs.org/core/index.html
The AIBS provides background information about all biological sciences,
   as well as updates on current research.

American Museum of Natural History
Central Park West at 79th Street
New York, NY 10024
(212) 769-5100
Web site: http://www.amnh.org/exhibitions/permanent/humanorigins
The American Museum of Natural History in New York City has a permanent collection dedicated to the understanding of human evolution. It
   also offers children's workshops and public education programs on
   such topics as fossil and genetic evidence for evolution and the possible interactions of Neanderthals and Homo sapiens.

Canadian Society for Ecology and Evolution (CSEE)
Department of Biology
Lakehead University
Thunder Bay, ON P7B 5E1
Canada
Web site: http://www.ecoevo.ca/en/index.htm
The CSEE promotes the study of ecology and evolution in Canada.

Genetics Society of America (GSA)
9650 Rockville Pike
Bethesda, MD 20814-3998

(301) 634-7300

Web site: http://www.genetics-gsa.org

The GSA strives to promote genetic education and interaction among geneticists and to advance genetic research.

Genetics Society of Canada (GSC)

The Snider's Web

59 Aulac Road

Aulac, NB E4L 2V6

Canada

(506) 536-1768

Web site: http://evol.mcmaster.ca/GSC/index.html

The GSC helps advance genetic research in Canada and communicate the results and implications of that research to the public.

National Center for Science Education (NCSE)

420 40th Street Suite 2

Oakland, CA 94609-2509

(510) 601-7203

Web site: http://ncseweb.org

The NCSE works to support scientific education in the public schools and to inform the public of challenges to teaching evolution in the classroom.

Public Broadcasting Service (PBS)

2100 Crystal Drive

Alexandria, VA 22202

Web site: http://www.pbs.org

PBS produces many videos, DVDs, and books that help explain evolution, extinction, and the importance of biodiversity.

Smithsonian National Museum of Natural History

10th Street and Constitution Avenue NW

Washington, DC 20560
(202) 633-1000
Web site: http://www.mnh.si.edu
The Smithsonian National Museum of Natural History has a permanent
    collection of fossils, as well as many temporary exhibits, to educate the
    public about Charles Darwin and the science of evolution.

Society for the Study of Evolution
Museum of Vertebrate Zoology
3101 Valley Life Sciences Building
Office 3101 VLSB
University of California, Berkeley
Berkeley, CA 94720
(510) 643-7711
Web site: http://www.evolutionsociety.org/index.asp
The Society for the Study of Evolution promotes the study of organic evolu-
    tion and publishes the journal Evolution.

Web Sites

Due to the changing nature of Internet links, Rosen Publishing has developed
an online list of Web sites related to the subject of this book. This site is
updated regularly. Please use this link to access the list:

http://www.rosenlinks.com/gen/evol

For Further Reading

Anderson, Margaret Jean. *Charles Darwin: Naturalist* (Great Minds of Science). Berkeley Heights, NJ: Enslow Publishers, 2008.

Butz, Steve. *The Bone Race: A Quest for Dinosaur Fossils*. Eagleville, PA: DNA Press, 2007.

DK Publishing. *Early Humans* (DK Eyewitness Books). New York, NY: DK Publishing, 2005.

Gamlin, Linda. *Evolution* (DK Eyewitness Books). New York, NY: DK Publishing, 2009.

Gibson, J. Phil. *Natural Selection* (Science Foundations). New York, NY: Chelsea House Publications, 2009.

Gordon, Sherri Mabry. *Evolution Debate: Darwinism vs. Intelligent Design* (Issues in Focus Today). Berkeley Heights, NJ: Enslow Publishers, 2009.

Heiligman, Deborah. *Charles and Emma: The Darwins' Leap of Faith*. New York, NY: Henry Holt & Company, 2008.

Kowalski, Kathiann. *Evolution on Trial: From the Scopes Monkey Case to Inherit the Wind*. Berkeley Heights, NJ: Enslow Publishers, 2009.

Leone, Bruno. *Origin: The Story of Charles Darwin*. Greensboro, NC: Morgan Reynolds, Inc., 2009.

Luongo, Charlotte. *Evolution* (Big Ideas in Science). Tarrytown, NY: Marshall Cavendish, 2009.

Raham, Gary. *Fossils* (The Restless Earth). New York, NY: Chelsea House Publications, 2009.

Shultz, Mark. *The Stuff of Life: A Graphic Guide to Genetics and DNA*. New York, NY: Hill and Wang, 2009.

Sloan, Christopher. *The Human Story: Our Evolution from Prehistoric Ancestors to Today*. Washington, DC: National Geographic Children's Books, 2004.

Spilsbury, Richard. *Journal of a Fossil Hunter: Fossils*. Chicago, IL: Heinemann-Raintree, 2005.

Van Gorp, Lynn. *Genetics* (Mission: Science). Minneapolis, MN: Compass Point Books, 2008.

Wagner, Vigi. *Endangered Species* (Opposing Viewpoints). Detroit, MI: Greenhaven Press, 2007.

Willett, Edward. *Genetics Demystified*. Maidenhead, Berkshire, England: McGraw-Hill Professional, 2005.

Winston, Robert. *Evolution Revolution*. New York, NY: DK Publishing, 2009.

Wood, A. J., and Clint Twist. *Charles Darwin and the Beagle Adventure*. Somerville, MA: Templar Books, 2009.

Zimmer, Carl. *Smithsonian Intimate Guide to Human Origins*. New York, NY: Harper Paperbacks, 2007.

Bibliography

AboutDarwin.com. "Evolution Before Darwin." February 10, 2008. Retrieved August 26, 2009 (http://www.aboutdarwin.com/literature/ Pre_Dar.html).

Bartlett, Kate. "Piltdown Man: Britain's Greatest Hoax." BBC, August 26, 2009 (http://www.bbc.co.uk/history/archaeology/excavations_ techniques/piltdown_man_01.shtml).

Berra, Tim. *Charles Darwin: The Concise Story of an Extraordinary Man.* Baltimore, MD: Johns Hopkins University Press, 2009.

Centers for Disease Control and Prevention. "Get Smart: Antibiotic Resistance Questions and Answers." August 26, 2009 (http:// www.cdc.gov/getsmart/antibiotic-use/anitbiotic-resistance-faqs.html).

Coyne, Jerry. *Why Evolution Is True.* New York, NY: Viking, 2009.

Daeschler, Edward, Neil Shubin, and Farish Jenkins. "A Devonian Tetrapod-like Fish and the Evolution of the Tetrapod Body Plan." *Nature*, April 6, 2006. Retrieved August 26, 2009 (http://www.nature.com/ nature/journal/v440/n7085/full/nature04639.html).

Davidson, J. E. "Rare Medical Conditions: Ellis-van Creveld Syndrome." *Associated Content*, December 21, 2007. Retrieved August 26, 2009 (http://www.associatedcontent.com/article/493187/rare_medical_ conditions_ellisvan_creveld.html?cat=52).

Ghiseli, Michael. "Nonsense in Schoolbooks: 'The Imaginary Lamarck'." Textbook League, August 26, 2009 (http://www.textbookleague. org/54marck.htm).

Leakey.com. "Leakey Legacy." August 26, 2009 (http://www.leakey.com).

Miller, Ken. "The Peppered Moth." August 26, 2009 (http://www. millerandlevine.com/km/evol/Moths/moths.html).

Minnesota State University, Mankato. "What Is Human Evolution?" August 26, 2009 (http://www.mnsu.edu/emuseum/biology/ humanevolution/humevol.html).

Morton, Carol. "Gene Linked to Beak Length in Darwin Finch." *Focus*, September 1, 2006. Retrieved August 26, 2009 (http://focus.hms.harvard.edu/2006/090106/genetics.shtml).

National Geographic News. ""MISSING LINK" FOUND: New Fossil Links Humans, Lemurs?" May 19, 2009. Retrieved August 26, 2009 (http://news.nationalgeographic.com/news/2009/05/090519-missing-link-found.html).

PBS. "Evolution Library." August 26, 2009 (http://www.pbs.org/wgbh/evolution/library/index.html).

PBS. "A Science Odyssey: Human Evolution." August 26, 2009 (http://www.pbs.org/wgbh/aso/tryit/evolution/#).

Ruse, Michael, and Joseph Travis, eds. *Evolution: The First Four Billion Years*. Cambridge, MA: Belknap Press of Harvard University Press, 2009.

University of California, Berkeley. "A Fish of a Different Color." Understanding Evolution, February 2006. Retrieved August 26, 2009 (http://evolution.berkeley.edu/evolibrary/news/060201_zebrafish).

University of California, Berkeley. "What Has the Head of a Crocodile and the Gills of a Fish?" Understanding Evolution, June 2009. Retrieved August 26, 2009 (http://evolution.berkeley.edu/evolibrary/news/060501_tiktaalik).

University of California Museum of Paleontology. "Understanding Evolution." August 26, 2009 (http://evolution.berkeley.edu/evolibrary/home.php).

University of Wisconsin–Madison Department of Bacteriology. "Bacterial Resistance to Antibiotics." August 26, 2009 (http://textbookofbacteriology.net/themicrobialworld/bactresanti.html).

Index

About the Author

Kristi Lew is the author of more than two dozen books on science for teachers and young adults. Fascinated with science from a young age, she studied biochemistry and genetics in college. Before she started writing full-time, she worked in genetics laboratories for more than ten years and taught high school science.

Photo Credits:

Cover (top) Don Emmert/AFP/Getty Images; cover (bottom), back cover, and interior © www.istockphoto.com/Gregory Spencer; p. 6 © Hubertus Kanus/TopFoto/The Image Works; p. 9 © Sean Sprague/The Image Works; pp. 10–11 Bounce/UpperCut Images/Getty Images; p. 12 © www.istockphoto.com/Warwick Lister-Kaye; p. 14 Randy Allbritton/Photodisc/Getty Images; pp. 16–17 © www.istockphoto.com/bobbieo; pp. 18–19 © Francis Leroy/Biocosmos/Photo Researchers, Inc.; p. 23 Mansell/Time & Life Pictures/Getty Images; p. 25 HIP/Art Resource, NY; p. 27 George Richmond/The Bridgeman Art Library/Getty Images; p. 29 Hulton Archive/Getty Images; p. 32 © SSPL/The Image Works; pp. 34–35 William Thomas Cain/Getty Images; pp. 38, 39 Wikipedia Commons; pp. 42–43 Mira Oberman/AFP/Getty Images; pp. 44–45 © Tierbild Okapia/Photo Researchers, Inc.; p. 46 © Volker Steger/Photo Researchers, Inc.; pp. 48–49 Zina Deretsky/National Science Foundation/Wikipedia; p. 51 © Franzen JL, Gingerich PD, Habersetzer J, Hurum JH, von Koenigswald W, et al. 2009 Complete Primate Skeleton from the Middle Eocene of Messel in Germany: Morphology and Paleobiology. PLoS ONE 4(5): e5723. doi:10.1371/journal.pone.0005723; p. 53 © Universal Images Group Limited/Alamy; p. 57 Harry Taylor/Dorling Kindersley/Getty Images; p. 59 Gianluigi Guercia/AFP/Getty Images; p. 61 © Des Bartlett/Photo Researchers, Inc.; pp. 62–63 © Daniel Herard/Photo Researchers, Inc.; pp. 66–67 © AP Images.

Designer: Nicole Russo; Editor: Kathy Kuhtz Campbell;
Photo Researcher: Amy Feinberg